Dominion Oluyadi

THE AMBASSADORS' DEVOTIONAL

Dominion Oluyadi

THE AMBASSADORS' DEVOTIONAL

...solution to juvenile delinquency

Blessed Hope Publishing

Imprint

Any brand names and product names mentioned in this book are subject to trademark, brand or patent protection and are trademarks or registered trademarks of their respective holders. The use of brand names, product names, common names, trade names, product descriptions etc. even without a particular marking in this work is in no way to be construed to mean that such names may be regarded as unrestricted in respect of trademark and brand protection legislation and could thus be used by anyone.

Cover image: www.ingimage.com

Publisher:
Blessed Hope Publishing
is a trademark of
International Book Market Service Ltd., member of OmniScriptum Publishing Group
17 Meldrum Street, Beau Bassin 71504, Mauritius
Printed at: see last page
ISBN: 978-613-7-89305-0

DOMINION OLUYADI
Vol 1
THE
AMBASSADORS
DEVOTIONAL
...solution to juvenile delinquency!

THE AMBASSADORS DEVOTIONAL PART 1

... Solution to juvenile delinquency!

TOC

ACKNOWLEDGEMENT

The Ambassadors Devotional is not a product of educational backlog, human wisdom, academic intelligence – or motivational projection.

This recipe is 100% a product of **God's direct inspiration and passion geared towards the urgent - rescue mission of teenagers and youths** from juvenile delinquency, ravaging the world!

The author is just a human tool chosen for this assignment [by virtue of his personal availability].

DEDICATION

The Ambassadors' Devotional

It's a literature dedicated to, Youths and Teenagers around the world, especially in Africa. Also to every institution or NGO whose vision and struggle, is passionately, geared towards reorientation and reformation of the juveniles around the world!

The Ambassadors Devotional is, "specially" customised in favour of **The Ambassadors Schools, Ota**, Nigeria. For the rare opportunity offered me to prove my mettle in this area such as –Juvenile Character Development!

Nonetheless, I also believe this book is as dedicated to every parent [including single parents], that must have been fighting via restless days and sleepless nights, to ensure their kids/wards turn out to be the best among their peers and mostly, to become positive role models to others – in their present and subsequent generations!

I feel the pain of every mother – especially the few among real mothers - who rather sacrifices whatever to ensure their juvenile, excel in life - your struggles will not end in vain!

"Every tears you have shed as parents will in return worth the efforts – as your baby child of yesterday emerge a positive, influential role model in adulthood, to the world around – and generations."

CONTENTS

INTRODUCTION

Many were asking if the first edition of **Juvenile Character Devotional** was going to be the last. Some said since they noted a tag bearing, "volume 1" – when is the second edition going to be out. Others kept their questions, opinions, and assumptions to themselves!

Personally, I knew the first volume was not going to be last, because of my passion for the African youths – but I was not sure, when the second and subsequent editions were going to be either!

Anyway, here is the second edition. Moreover, I believe the publication of this edition is going to [of no doubt] cushion the effect of everyone's doubt as to – if, if, if, etc.

Questions that had ever arose, owing to the gap between the first and second shall be resolved here.

Another issue is, you may likely find what you could have thought was missing in the first edition.

I will also want to build more on some of the issues, stories, observations, etc., that was made in the first edition. This is not because I lack content but just that, there ought to be certain clarifications of, certain clauses that I could have delved into [in depth], but for time constrain, based on the time - target.

NOTE:

Every edition is meant to serve for a quarter – I mean for three months at a stretch. The idea is so each juvenile could have the more opportunity of assimilating the contents in each edition productively!

Also, this edition is titled after **The Ambassador's School,** as a support to the founders' vision towards raising young ambassadors capable of reforming the world – by first being reformed, via character values!

In conclusion, I believe you will find the second edition also interesting like as the first or possibly (more interesting] better - depending on your expectation.

Welcome to **World's Greatest Juvenile World**!

Dominion D. Oluyadi

February 2nd, 2020

Lagos.

Nigeria.

Africa.

Day 1

Topic: DO YOU HAVE BRAIN

How will you feel if your bosom friend should ask you the above question - do you have brain?

The fact is we all have our individual opinion in every issue or matter that transpires before us. We have different ears in terms of trying words and thoughts. However, the bottom, line is - what's your take on the issue here? What will be your personal response, if the above question is directed at you, without any pre-information, adequate preparation, presumption or permutation as regards the subject matter?

The fact down here must, not be treated with levity. The weight of the question carries a great gravity that calls for serious meditation, critical analyses and rational review.

As long as the book centers on the juvenile, I am appealing to the mind of each teenager and youth to take this question seriously. In fact, I advise you take the question **"do you have a brain"** as a challenging puzzle that is capable of fetching you an academic scholarship or national recommendation which possesses inherent international recognition and other values, even at your juvenile period in life, among your age categories and academic contemporaries around the world. Moreover, to neglect this challenging question is to also further relegate your mental capacity to the normal, common – youth's mental status- quo! A thought that rather believe –what will be will be!

To become special in life, you must be prepared to do impossible things, because **it takes a degree of special mental-ability to enjoy special immunity in the society**. The normal thinking will only fetch normal results but [abnormal yet] radical, analytical – fact-finding thinking will shoot you beyond the skies and stars.

This sort of question ought to challenge your juvenile credibility to withstand whatever is out to play down on your mental dignity and juvenile ability to unravel the intelligence hidden behind the test thrown at you, both now and forever!

Day 2

Topic: **WHAT'S IN YOUR BRAIN**

The title of today's lecture may sound similar to the first. Nevertheless, this rather sound more of a probing question than that of the first, which was a challenging one.

Let me help you breakdown the above title.

The simplicity of the question is asking after **your brain contents**! In other words, the following question should help you unravel the realities inherent your personal brain-contents.

Now let me help you understand the question better. For instance, whenever you pick up a novel. Flip over the introduction page, or preface. The next page normally reads; "table of contents".

The table of contents literately unveils the contents of the book by virtue of each chapter's heading or title. In other words, the table of contents is the first insight you require to access the full book. It is from the table of contents of each book you can imagine the nature, structure and direction of such in terms of overall information inherent the literature. One other information the table of contents offers you is - it affords you with the liberty of the choice to pick on the chapter you desire to read before others. This time you are not constrain or tied to follow the table of contents according to it's sequential order. You may decide to read chapter four before reading chapter one, etc. it all depends on your take per time.

In the same vein, I want you list out your personal brain contents with brevity.

In other words, **"what service can your brain offer the world"?**

Here is another example:

My Personal Brain Contents

- I am a thought developer
- I write books for myself
- I write books for people/organisations
- I do proofreading service
- I offer lectures on business/ leadership
- I offer lectures on juvenile/leadership character
- I develop resource materials for conferences, etc.

From the above example you should be able to understand what I mean by the question that serves as the topic for this chapter- **what is in your brain**!!!

Largely, the end user, and not just the manufacturer who intend to convince the user best describe the functionality of a product. You should be able to identify your abilities and special abilities than anyone else.

What is in your brain unveils your personal ability to define your identity with brevity and confidence. You can be called upon to say what you're capable of doing with little or without supervision, this is how many youths have gained prominence, being given rare opportunities to prove their relevance. **Understanding and development of personal talent into special ability opens door for unexpected opportunity** – yet, to experience such – you must live ready! The difference between getting ready and living ready is:

- Those who get ready = unprepared folks
- Those who live ready = fully prepared folks

The fact about life reality is; the world is looking for those who are already prepared – hence no one has the luxury of time to waste, by waiting for those who are just trying to get prepared.

Apparently – **if you're not prepared you won't also be preferred. The world is on a fast lane, only the prepared are permitted to drive along such space [to avoid accidents].** In other words, the world preferred the prepared only!

Day 3

Topic: PERSONAL BRAIN CONTENT

I believe from the last chapter you must have understood the treasures inherent your personal brain [contents]?

Your assignment in this chapter is quite simple.
Cut out a blank paper, or draw a graph on your PC with the title in accordance with the above topic.
Make a project of it. Take your time to itemize what you believe your brain can do, or the services you know yourself can render to humanity. You may not need to end the documentation or itemization at a go, but you just open up the page and pay attention to what details you document in there.
You can also duplicate such documentation, by placing the compilation on your personal room door, bathroom door, library shelve frame, etc, a place you know is conspicuous enough for you to observe it as you go on daily - you must be serious with this project. Believe me for the first time this new measure will help you do self-mental evaluation.

This exercise is bound to further, reinforce your personal discipline by focusing on developing your mentality and juvenile capacity. Such assignment will help you place value on your life by the unique value you place on each moment and time you spend in "your entire lifetime!"

Day 4

Topic: YOU HAVE A BRAIN

At this junction, it is necessary for us to consult the expert on brain study and makeup, for correct/current information and further, relevant education.

Each time one, or people allow the professionals handle issues that requires professionalism, the best of information and knowledge surrounding such topic will always be unveiled without much ado, because, facts will be made available without struggle.

You cannot think or assume you could conclude on brain as subject matter without consulting a neurosurgeon, just as you cannot conclude on childbearing subject without involving the gynaecologist – in the same vein – a professional neurosurgeon must be brought on board, to widen our horizon on the human brain and the topic in focus!

The next portion of this chapter is as documented by **Ben Carson, MD – A very popular black American**

Neurosurgeon, who has operated on thousands of brains successfully:

- *"Inside each human brain are approximately 86 billion neurons interconnected by more than 100 trillion synapses (estimated since no one has counted them all yet), which science has only barely begun to understand.*
- *You brain started developing almost immediately after conception. During the first month of your mother's pregnancy, your body was creating neurons at the rate of about 400 million per day.*
- *Your brain generates electricity constantly, enough every walking minute to keep a low - wattage light bulb fully lit. So when you say, that's a bright idea, your statement could be literally as well as figuratively true.*
- *Sensory signals move along an alpha motor neuron in your spinal cord at 268 million per hour (mph). This is the fastest transmission of this type in the body. Skin sensory receptors, which travel at about 1 mph, are among the slowest in the body because they do not have myelin sheath, which would insulate them and boost their speed.*
- *The brain of the normal twenty year old human possess 100,000 miles of myelin – covered nerve fibres.*

- *Your brain can feel no pain because it has no pain receptors. The organ that controls the whole nervous system and it cannot feel pain! This is why we can operate on the brain without worrying about the pain level of the patient. It's also the reason why we can perform surgery on people who are awake, as they feel absolutely nothing.*
- *Harvard university neuroscientist Jeff Lichtman, who is attempting to map the brain, has calculated that several million pet bytes of data storage would be needed to index the entire human brain.*
- *When scientists try to quantify the capacity of the human brain, the number get so high that we can't get our minds around them.* ***The potential of your mind is literally mindboggling.****"*

Culled from; **YOU HAVE A BRAIN [ZONDERVAN .COM]**

Day 5

Topic: **MANAGE YOUR BRAIN**

***Welcome to day five*!**

My dear young personality, I know you might be wondering all this while, why on earth; I have been dwelling on the brain topic (after all there are a thousand and one issues affecting the juvenile world], Why brain?

Merriam Webster dictionary defines brain as the organ of the body in the head that connects:

Functions

Movements

Sensations

Thoughts

The ability to think

A very intelligent person

Full definition

The portion of the vertebrate central nervous system enclosed in the skull. And continuous with the spinal cord through the foreman megrim that is composed of neuron and supporting and nutritive structures, (such as glair) and that integrate sensory information from inside and outside the body in controlling autonomic function) such as heart beat and respiration, in coordination and directing correlated of learning.

In a bid to understand the management of your brain, let's consider the following highlight [as boldly written above]:

- Functions
- Movements
- Sensations
- Thoughts

The productive use of the above highlight is what culminates in brain management.

1. If your brain must **function** maximally, then you must engage such in line with what God created it for – "thinking".

2. **Movement** – the movement of your brain changes position from time to time depending on your thinking sequence, [which must be positive, of course]!
3. **Sensation** – brain sensation is the ability to feel things through your physical senses.
4. **Thought** - thoughts are the processes by which your brain performs usefully, by generating ideas, planning, perceptions, etc. Such activities help your brain experience the process of thinking through issues before drawing conclusion.

In conclusion,

The product of your personal thinking [including your secret thoughts], are practically the realities of your mental investment.

Therefore, when I said manage your brain – I mean to say-manage your mind. I define mind as-

Mental

Investment

Notable

Developments

Your personal line of **mental investment** is what determines notable developments.

Notable development is the hallmark of geniuses - very intelligent people, because they engage their brains (minds) to think, reason, and proffer solutions to the challenges beclouding humanity in different sphere and capacities.

- When you begin to manage your brain (well), as a juvenile, today – you're sure of a successful future as you graduate into adulthood.
- When you manage your brain well, you must be up reading, while others are oversleeping their lives away.
- When you manage your brain well – you're bound to become one of the solution generators in your generation!
- When you manage your brain well – you are likely to turn out to be your nation's helper - that makes you a hero!

Here is my question to you: are you prepared to manage your brain well? **Then prove such by adding value to your stay and education at the Ambassadors' school today!**

Day 6

Topic: **YOUR LIFE'S VISION**

In the first devotion I made mention of vision briefly while talking about **Dream Building** in page 37. [You could get such to know the angle I am driving at here].

In the next few days, I will like to write [or speak to you] extensively on vision.

Vision is one of the avenues that help one in productive brain management.

I have, through sincere observation come to understand that **lack of vision is the major reason behind juvenile character deficiencies** around the world.

If you miss the vision of your personal life, you will definitely be pursuing another person's vision.

To lack your own vision is to lack your own future - to lack your own future is to fight for other people's future, unknowingly = failure!

Vision is what you crave for; because in such contains your whole life evolvement from phase to phase. Your life at a certain stage, or at some point receives wings [of the eagle] to fly above your peers who lacks such visionary hype and height.

Every genuine ambassador who is out to represent an organisation, institution or nation must definitely possess a distinctive vision – vision is what gives one the clarity of direction in any given assignment. Without a clear-cut vision, there will always be confusion. Confusion is the reason for error. Compounded errors gradually initiate horror.

It's of utmost importance that every juvenile equip himself/herself with productivity - oriented vision at a very prime age. Such juvenile's life, with visionary mentality & fortification helps one beat down juvenile distractions in life! **Accessibility to personal vision for life, at a very early stage, prepares you for leadership even prior to your leadership positioning in life. Such makes you reason beyond your natural age. It develops your mental capacity for proactive thinking.**

Vision is one of the disparities between academically successful student and academic failure. It's also same for failed leadership and the successful one.

TODAY

IS

REVISION

The teacher is mean to do a revision after every six days of the study of the devotional with the students.

Each one of the students, is expected to make contribute during such exercise [by a way of question or answer].

Day 7th

Topic: DEFINITION OF VISION

The **ability to see**; sight or eyesight, something that you **imagine** a picture that you see in your **mind**.

Something you see or dream especially as part of a religious supernatural experience.

From the above definition, let us pick on the words painted boldly.

Ability to see

I like this, ability to see! Please understand not we all see. Especially among young peers, you should remember sometimes you people argue about the reality of what you see at times, because you are naturally expected, to see differently.

What do I mean?

Should you all be asked, to describe what you claim to see exactly – you all must definitely come up with different descriptions. The question is why different descriptions; it is because your individual visual ability is different from each other's. Our individual observation capacity comes with disparity

More also, if the teacher is to mark your script after each one's [submission of his/her] description, definitely the grades will not be same except you spy at each other's answer sheet!

The question is what is responsible for each one's experience?

Individual ability to see

We don't have the same visual ability when it comes to visual expression.

Another fact responsible for this is -

There are three types of eyes

- The eyes that looks
- The eyes that sees
- The eyes that sees clearer

Capacity to see, clearer, varies from person to person. Hence we can't all have or run the same vision in life. **A true ambassador cannot be experiencing impaired vision and still expect to perform maximally. Impaired vision degenerates into frustration, because it reduces the productivity and capacities of the affected fellow to minimal achievement when it comes to work appraisal and performance evaluation**.

One thing is to be mentally loaded, yet physically limited or relegated sort of, because of visually impaired difficulty.

Impaired vision will not become your lot in life!

Day 8

Topic: DEFINITION OF VISION [2]

Here is the second reason, which determines the expression of what you claim to see - **imagination**.

Imagination is the formation of mental picture on your mind. What does it imply?

Those who **look** are in the category of those who want to **feed their eyes**.

Those who **imagine** are in the category of those who want to **feed their minds**.

Therefore, should you belong to the second group, it means you are seeing beyond your physical eyes could. It also means you are seeing through whatever your eyes looks or sees per time!

DREAM
Because I have written a bit on dream in the first juvenile character devotional, I will not want to dwell on it here, so I will not be repeating myself.

I am going to provide you with the dictionary definition only:
"Series of the thoughts, vision or seeking that happen during sleep
An idea that is created in your imagination.
Something that, you have waited very much to do, be or have for a long time."

Supernatural experience
The summary of the above; boils down to God showing you certain, yet unknown things!
Anything supernatural means – something that is not natural something divine. For instance;
Human being is natural
God is supernatural [Spirit being].

Ambition sometimes, may come naturally, based on one's frequent thought line or following addiction to a certain role model in one of the societies of the world. Nevertheless, vision, is contrary to ambition, because God – human creator, orchestrates vision. Hence, vision is supernatural in terms of accessibility and reality.

Another truth is you can give yourself ambition but you can't give yourself vision – only God gives vision

Day 9

Topic: WHAT IS VISION

I have been able to break down Merriam Webster - dictionary definition for you. Now permit me to define vision for you in applicable way.

Short story on vision

A little girl was on a cruise ship, she and her dad were standing on the deck. The day was beautiful and clear. The sky above was clear enough for everyone's visual clarity.

Nevertheless, this little girl was said to stand upon her toes, yet she could not see far off. Then, the dad lifted her up on his shoulders, after a short while she exclaimed in excitement:

"Daddy, I can see farther beyond my eyes can look"

I define vision as follows -

- Vision is the ability to see beyond what the eyes can look
- Vision is the accessibility to the future, today

- Vision is breaking the barrier of limitation from human visualisation.
- Vision is the ability to capture your personal future from a single picture
- Vision comprehends your personal purpose – description with distinction
- Vision is ability to grasp your personal destination in life with precision
- Vision is supernatural accessibility to your destiny details with clarity of understanding.
- Vision is the revelation of your supernatural identity in humanity
- Vision is the blue print of your life details in clear print.
- Vision is having a sure direction without confusion
- Vision is the authencity of your personality in humanity

To understand the details from the above highlights then you need to go over such once or twice, to sift out detailed information inherent the contents.

Day 10

Topic: DO I NEED VISION

Today's devotional resource opens up with the question; **"Do I need vision?"**

Yes! You truly need vision!

One of the reasons for juvenile delinquency in the world today is because, about 90% of teenagers and youths lack direction for their lives!

Just like the young girl, whose father lifted up above himself and everyone on the ship deck, before she was able to see farther, than her physical eyes could - you cannot see your tomorrow today and still allow yourself to be short sighted.

In the next few days, I will be telling you simple reasons why you need vision.

I promise you, - it won't be boring.

I am all out to work on your brain in this edition. Once your brain is able to grasp the picture I will be showing you, you're sure to experience a great future. **Knowing what you need helps you discard what you don't - promptly**!

Day 11

Topic: ***VISION UNVEILS YOUR IDENTITY***

I am going to put you on a horse race from today's lecture.

Baby lion story

There was a story I learnt as narrated to Dr. Myles Munroe [of blessed memory], a community head equally told it him.

It was about a baby lion that was picked up by one of the old hunters in the community - in one of such hunting game. He brought home the baby lion after he was sure the mother wasn't coming for him, or anywhere near the scene.

The baby lion was integrated into the sheepfold. After few days he began to blend with sheep's character, he ate their kind of food, played their kind of games and did things in common with his new sheep-family [though, originally he wasn't one; but life is where you find it].

Occasionally, while in the company of the sheep each time they are out to graze. After grazing, they retire to a certain riverbank where they normally drink water. Frightening enough, there was this big lion, which sometimes roar from across side of the river. Just as you know there is no sheep nor animal that is not threatened at the roar of the lion. When the lion roared - the sheep took to their heels, it was a survival of the fittest experience.

There came a day, the baby lion was the first to outrun the sheep siblings to the river, surprising to the young lion on arrival at the riverbank. As he overlaps the water, he saw the image of himself on the water and it looks exactly like that of the big lion. Then he paused for a while because he was a bit puzzled. He was of the opinion it must have been the big lion. Nonetheless, he played along with the sheep siblings on their arrival few seconds later. Yet, he was pondering upon the picture he saw prior to his sheep-siblings arrival.

Few weeks later, they were at the riverbank and the big lion roared as usual. While others took to their heels - he boldly swam across, even though his attitude was just like that of the sheep where he was adopted – his physical and outward appearance was that of a lion. However, the big lion did not hurt but gave him warm welcome. As the big lion, turns away from the water bank and head towards the forest. He waited a while, wondering and gazing at the young lion, as he looked behind considering whether to follow the big lion or return to his sheep family. Eventually he decided to follow the big lion to start a new life, **having found his identity – a lion!**

REALITY OF IDENTITY

- Identity makes you **original**
- Identity makes you **bold**
- Identity shows you your **class**
- Identity reveals your true **nature**
- Identity helps you discover **purpose**
- Identity repositions your **ideology**
- Identity establishes your true **identity in reality**
- Identity defines your **personality**

Just like the young lion – who now discovered lions crack bones, while sheep feed on grass.

Identity helps you crack bones - solving great tasks.

- Lions live in the jungle where it's about survival of the fittest, unlike sheep that depends and are at the mercy of humans for survival in life. Survival in life is by taking personal responsibility.
- Lions are at liberty to hunt down whatever animal at whatever time of the day – sheep have no liberty, they

don't have their own mind or either could make any meaningful decision

- Lions we are told, lives longer than sheep's - why humans are free to hunt down the sheep anytime and anyhow. Have you heard of where lions are hunted down [in a community] by humans without resistance?

Here is the question:
From the above context, which of the animals will you rather chose to become if you were created an animal?
What's your choice among the two, that you believe your identity is going to be in life?

Day 12

Topic: VISION DICTATES YOUR DIRECTION

Have you ever read or heard of a ship's survival in a stormy weather [on the sea], without a rudder?

Did anyone ever told you an airplane survived after losing communication, synergy - with the control tower?

In the same vein, you cannot successfully develop your juvenile character adventure, successfully without a specialized direction in life. To develop a specialized direction in life [just like the ship and aeroplane]; you will always require vision. Vision is the compass of destiny.

For instance, imagine you're on board a chattered vehicle and the driver ask about the direction of the journey so he could set up the GPS, but You're saying - I don't know?

Or, let's say you are on board a chattered cab, and you immediately gave the driver the address to where you're heading, only for you to begin to hear the GPS announcer mention a route contrary to your designated destination. You're or likely to find yourself in a wrong location at the end of such journey, should you continue on such trip.

Nevertheless, when the right direction is programmed into goggle map, the programmed- announcer is bound to mention names and places it's familiar with, based on the direction you programme into it.

Companions of programmed direction

For every addressed direction - the following companions are, immediately factored in:

- Definition – being able to ascertain your journey
- Attention – ability to focus on the journey
- Observation – taking notice of things on your journey
- Clarification – being full of confidence in your journey
- Destination – your arrival in the journey-as planned

With such sequence in place, your confidence is aroused.

TODAY

IS

REVISION

Day 13

Topic: ***BUYERS & SELLERS WORLD***

In case, you are wondering what the correlation between business and character is - I am just trying to open your eyes to the reality of business availability in our society and how it could further arouse your mental reasoning productively, when mixed up with quality character.

We are living in a world that is a cohabitation of buyers and sellers. No one survives in the world without buying or selling!

Sellers dictate the prices of commodities. Buyers purchase based on decision of sellers, which comprises of type of commodities, etc. For instance, look around you, the vehicles, telecommunication, phone accessories, electricity, electrical appliances, domestic utensils, etc.

First, which one of these is manufactured in Africa? We all buyer and sell, period. Nevertheless, the buyers are at the mercy of sellers.

Only sellers dictate what is sold, the amount it's sold, who to sell to and location for sale per time.

The buyers have lesser choice or control over this fact. Here is wisdom; sellers become richer, while buyers become poorer. Whatever you buy reduces your bank account balance. In addition, whatever you sell [should you be among sellers], increases your account balance.

My observation is – if you're not among the sellers, you're bound to end up poor. I have experimented what I am teaching you. A certain year, I was paid a million naira as fee for sealing a deal. I began to withdraw the money bit by bit. Few months after I became broke, why? Because I was only buying, I was not selling! Continual withdrawal without savings reduces income.

Each time a business transaction takes place anywhere around the world - the seller benefits more, for the account balance of seller increases at the detriment of that of the buyer [which reduces].

What sense am I making here? My dear youngster, if you don't have what you are selling, you will become poor.

This is why you must use your brain. You may be living on your parents or other people's purses today, such opportunities will never last forever.

While such opportunities persist, you must wake up now! Using your brain helps you focus more on your studies and academic pursuits with addiction – such addiction helps you avoid the plaque called: distraction, [which is common with teenagers and youths]. Moreover, true ambassadors are known to be more dedicated to the course or core business of the organisation they represent per time. You don't need to wait until you're a graduate before constructing the bridge to your future – today. What you're good at today may equally to turn out to become your breakthrough-product tomorrow. While others are submitting applications here and there and getting frustrated, you're just having fun – because you have been able to master a certain skill, idea, thought line, etc. in your school days. Rather than becoming a liability to your parents who invested fortune into your education, believing you're sure to triumph – but here you're bothering them daily for transport fair – when are they going to enjoy parental rest?

This will not be your portion!

Accepting personal responsibility at a young age helps position such juvenile in a good position to help others later in life.

This is why you must task your brain to think like a true ambassador – who proffers solution by adding living a value added life.

Day 14

Topic: **ARE YOU LOSING**

When you see or hear a question like this, it sometimes sounds confusing, except you're taken through the question word by word.

You are losing:

- Every time you sit before the local television, and the telecast does not benefit your life – you're losing! What are you loosing – **Time**!
- When you contribute to the criticism sponsored by a group, or your peers who are fond of gossiping = you're losing! Losing what – you're losing **personal energy** you ought to expend on something better.
- Every moment you find yourself on social media, browsing and smiling. As long as what you're watching is not adding any value to your life - you're losing! Losing what – loosing **data** – data is money.

The loss of data is same with the loss of money, it does not matter if it's your money or someone else.

- To see off your friend/classmate to his/her friend's - place in the name of hangout. Only to discuss about the fashion in vogue, such as: clothes, shoes, phones, jewelleries, music, films, etc. you're losing!

What are you losing?

You're losing **focus**!

Those things in vogue will not add to your life. No! Not valuable to your life, at least not for now, because they are not part of your education and academic vitalities.

- Anytime you intentionally, or partially tell a lie, to safe your face or telling such to defend your friend or classmate – you're losing - your **juvenile character**.

Talking about character

Someone said, and I quote:

"When a man lose wealth

He has lost nothing

When a man lose health

He has lost something

But, when a man lose is character

He has lost everything"

- Each time you gaze at what your peers are putting on, type of cars their parents are driving, nor the kind of phones they bring to school, etc - you're losing! What are you loosing!

You are losing your **emotions**!

It makes no sense thinking about what your parents cannot afford at least for now. The most important affordability is your education. When you pull through school, you may be the one to shower your parents with such – as a way of reward.

Boredom is going to drain your blood if you continue to dissipate energy on mundane thoughts and things, such could lead to sickness, and sickness sometimes leads to death. You must learn to be contented with what your parents could afford for now - believe me, the reason your parents lack such things now is as to curtail your excesses and [possible] frivolities – such as capable of making youths derail in meaningful life pursuits. Many families are victims of such experience today.

You won't be surprise when those things begin to come later!

Day 15

Topic: YOU ARE LOSING

I Learnt of, a fourteen-year-old boy who committed suicide in the year 2019.

The footnote discovered at his death place said – he committed suicide because his girlfriend left him!

What an aberration - an underage to die for love? What did such immature boy knew about love. This sort of juvenile delinquency is as a result of, lack of periodic student's attitude seminars in schools.

Whatever idea that young boy was having is lost!

Lost what?

Lost out of eternity. Anyone who commits suicide will always end up in hell fire!

- When you find yourself over sleeping – you're losing

What are you losing?

You're losing **potentials & strength**

This is why those who oversleep are usually lazy, because they expend their strength on oversleeping. Have you heard of the story of Jonah?

How his oversleeping made others lose their goods and wealth [because of his disobedience to God].

- Anytime your observation, your affection or addiction for food is becoming too much – you're losing!

What are you loosing?

You're likely to lose **your birthright** like Esau!

- Don't be free with other people's food - a lot of children are usually bewitched through such careless, caution less attitude [as vulnerable avenue]!
- In case, you're easily temperamental, because you were tempted to get angry over little provocation

You're losing!

You're losing your **self control**. Lack of self-control turns people into fools, because other people intentionally used their temper against them – knowing they are going to fall for such.

- Do you talk too much?

If you talk too much, you're losing

What are you losing?

You're losing your **secrets**. People love to engage whoever is a talkative in unnecessary discussion so as to get secret information from them. This is why many lousy talkers have landed themselves into trouble – including youths.

Negative habits in a juvenile will always remain negative habits when such turn adult. When such habits could no longer be curtailed – it will eventually result into public humiliation!

Day 16

Topic: ***ARE YOU GAINING***

- Each time you spend data on carrying out a knowledge based research - you are gaining

What are you gaining?

You're gaining **knowledge**

- Each time you discover something new about your line of education you're gaining

What are you gaining?

You're gaining **information**

- Every information you're privileged to access, which is in line with your career.

You're gaining?

What re you gaining?

You're gaining by leveraging on one of the **secrets of leadership**. The secret behind the making of leaders is the acquisition of information ahead of others, especially current information.

- The moment you find yourself obeying your parent's instruction in line with moral structure, you're gaining

What are you gaining?

You're gaining the **future**.

"Moral instructions are the highway to distinction in life"

- When a young person forms the habit of standing up for elders , especially in public places such is gaining

What is the gain?

Such is saving earned-respect for **future honour**!

Good habits and moral upbringing are like seed sown, which later becomes mighty tree. The more of such seeds sown the more the trees are grown until such becomes a forest - the forest experience is where the dividends for moral upbringing lie in wait for the juveniles when they turn adults!

Day 17

Topic: **DON'T YOU THINK**

You know some questions sound funny. When someone ask if you're thinking, you might be thinking if the person does think too, if not he should know already, that, everybody thinks.

Should the above correspond with your subscription, I would not say you were wrong or right. However, at the end of this lecture today, you should know where you stand between wrong [thinking] and right [thinking].

Story on Bill

Several years ago, a woman in America was calling out the name of her son around the house, when she discovered his unavailability [so she assumed].

After she had exhausted her search, and it seemed such effort ended in futility. She displayed a new strategy by screaming;

Bill, Bill, Bill.

Where are you?

Bill, Bill, Bill!!!

After few minutes, (I supposed] Bill roared when he sensed a sort of apprehension from the intonation of the mum).

Bill responded, angrily,

Yes mum, said Bill.

Where are you, asked the mum "I am thinking, mum, don't you think"

Few years after such mother and child reactions-

The young man turns out to be Bill Gates

The product of his thought turns out to be Microsoft!

The argument about what you think and when you think is not as important as the proof you have to show the world of your thinking exercises and efforts – when you become successful in life! It is not easy to convince anyone that you're thinking. Whether you're thinking or pretend to be thinking, the end product of your thought is what justifies your thinking exercise. As you add to the list of successful entrepreneurs, politicians, doctors, pilots, lawyers, or leading in your chosen field – then, it will be stupid for anyone to doubt your backlog of thinking years, because of your present status!

Day 18

Topic: **DO YOU REALLY THINK**

I know you should by this time understand the nature of my question.

Of course, I know you have been thinking.

Nevertheless, I challenged you to show me the proof of what you have been thinking.

Microsoft is the tangible proof of Bill Gates years of thinking. When your thoughts begin to generate or give birth to tangible products, then, no one will ask you if you have been thinking, because every product speaks for the manufacturer.

Each time you lay hold on a product you may not necessarily check the manufacturer's identity. But after a while, may be days, weeks, or months, when you begin to witness the positive or negative effects of such product [in your life], then you're most likely going to check the manufacturer's identity and product's pedigrees, before recommending or condemning such to someone close to you.

The positive effectiveness of each product is the invincible voice of the manufacturer.

Many among Africans may not seem to be able to identify Bill Gates as a person, but the Microsoft products are now so common everywhere around the world because of its diverse relevance.

That is the clear example of what human thinking could achieve.

If you begin to develop your thinking line, or reasoning pattern towards the positive, you too are likely to generate better software than what Bill Gates' thinking of yesterday is driving, in today world.

Just as I have told you before now - not until your thinking begins to generate a tangible product or relevant service to humanity - you may never become relevant in your generation, let alone subsequent generations.

If you lack capacity, you won't be needed in the city.

I see the word capacity as a compound word;

Capability – **city.**

"Human thinking capabilities are the results of all tangible developments which make up each city of the world"

Therefore the mental capabilities of each human is unlimited in terms of potential – yet it is individual's responsibility to widen his horizon via his capacity to think; behind, before, beneath - beyond whatever others [before him] could have generated in terms of mental possibility!

We shall be looking at three categories of thinking the next three days!

I believe your pattern of reasoning must definitely change for the better before the end of this devotional. Except you refuse to free your mind.

Knowledge transference is never by force but by choice. Once the passion is there, the flow of virtues can't be resisted in conversation or communication. Every book is a dialogue between the writer [speaker] and the reader [audience]. Yet, concentration is required.

TODAY

IS

REVISION

Day 19

Topic: MEDIOCRITY THINKING

We all humans are involved in the business of thinking on daily bases. Every time you find yourself lost in some somewhat [thought], you are in the business of thinking.

Nevertheless, your frequent line of thought and mine is what determine how we end up in life, largely.

Mediocrity - I define via following examples:

- Now let me be frank with you, each time the focus of your thought centers on mundane things, it therefore means, your life is, geared towards mundane things.
- For instance, when a young woman think or dream about the best clothes, shoes, jewelleries, and all sorts of materialistic drive, that is what such will definitely attract to her life and also end up becoming in life.
- Few years down the line in life while your peers with you in school [today], are becoming founders of institutions and leaders in major organizations and living and leading meaningful life [tomorrow].

You are going to be seen having enough clothes, shoes, and jewelleries, yet without a meaningful life – why, your thought life was based on materialism, therefore that becomes your lot.

- One fact about materialism, especially the ones in vogue is they all have their expiring dates. I mean they soon become old fashion. It will then dawn on you that you have wasted your mental energy on things that lack durability, importance and humanity-benefit-oriented.

In case you fall into these categories, it's not too late – you can reposition your future by repositioning your line of thought today.

Day 20

Topic: CREATIVE & PRODUCTIVE THINKING

The above pair may sound same at the end of each spelling and pronunciation, yet they have many disparities.

Creative thinking

This has to do with – searching for a way out in a situation, a problematic situation on ground. **Creative thinking is the ability to proffer curative solution that carries the content that deem fit, with precision**. Nevertheless, the ability to generate solution to challenging situation is rooted in the passion one possesses towards positive change. Every renowned inventor was once known to be one of those who reacted against the status quo in a certain field by very strong criticism, prior to the promulgation of their own products and arrival of their personalities - via public acceptability.

Creative thinking often radically generates controversy at it's inception of introduction, after a while the new wave becomes a trend. Therefore, creative thinking is not totally about the introduction of something new – rather such ideology could rather help generate different ideology that is capable of challenging the old system or product until it succeed to relegate such. For instance – there was a time **Bluetooth** was the major means of transferring data – in the 21st century, quite more new, vibrant technological products are been introduced.

Humanity is specie that lacks of satisfaction! Man will always want more. In addition, as long as man cannot be satisfied by what is readily available, hence inventions and innovations will continue to thrive without experiencing extinction!

My dear youngster, don't be afraid – be bold enough to contribute your quota while you are yet young because as you grow into adulthood, quite many distractions are capable of choking your ideas, before enjoying daylight.

I must also let you know this fact of life - **for every idea generated – there are consumers of such products even, prior to its consummation awareness of such by it's manufacturer!** However, it will amaze you that while you are sleeping with your fantastic idea – someone somewhere has produced exactly same without having any pre-information of yours; idea is not to be hoard but to be shared!

Productive thinking

The simple reality behind productive thinking is the ability to create impact from [or with], that which is created to the point of generating profits – return on investment [**ROI**].

This is why majority of leaders skilful in creative and productive thinking are usually absorbed into the **strategy and planning department** of a well structured organization.

These set of leaders are the ones, responsible [mainly] for driving the organisation into enviable future.

Organized creative and productive thinking, are products of purpose – oriented reasoning, and not materialism – driven thoughts. Check yourself with this truth and see if you measure up or not. Be sincere in your judgement – it's about you!

Purpose - oriented reasoning, places demand on every individual, with understanding to that effect. One of such demands is the attitude of living a purpose-driven life. For instance, it is expected of every serious minded student to study his books with little or no supervision. Such discipline initiative is, basically purpose driven!

DAY 21

Topic: BORN GREAT

We have been hearing about great people and events. My dear youngster, the truth is everyone is born with potential for greatness. Why did I say so, because the creator of the universe created each one special, with inherent potential - and such potential when excavated - will in turn be invested into building up the world, via various transformational strategies and appropriate avenues?

Challenges

One thing is to be born great, another is to become great. However, greatness possibility comes with several challenges. The process for becoming great forbids the following:

- You cannot be oversleeping and think you will ever become great.
- You cannot be a phone addict and think such addiction will culminate in greatness. The challenge opposing your greatness is what you do with your today, will determine if you will ever become great tomorrow:

Instructions

Should you be interested in greatness, then apply yourself to the following instructions.

Adherence to reasonable instruction is your connection to distinction.

Self-discovery

It is your responsibility to discover who you are. If you do not know who you are, you may not equally appreciate what you have; hence, you lack personal recognition of your potential and value for existence.

For instance, look around your house, there are different electrical appliances each performs a different function.

The function each performs makes such unique. For instance:

- Refrigerator supplies cold water
- Air conditioner suppliers chilled weather
- Television supplies visual entertainment
- The pressing iron functions by making your dresses appear neat and acceptable each, etc

The manufacturer that way built each of the items' function. Hence, each could not perform otherwise.

The question is; what were you manufactured for?

The same way you and your family members, often take time to study each electrical appliance manual before deploying such accordingly - in the same vein **it is your personal responsibility to find out your personal function on earth** - that's self-discovery!

Day 22

Topic: BORN GREAT II

"What's Your Destination?"

You must understand the subject of destination clearly, if you must also grasp the instruction of greatness deeply.

There is always a crowd at each nation's airport, especially during festive seasons. Some are flying in and some are flying out. Every five minutes, maximally, the announcer mentions a flying out airplane.

Nevertheless, as many as the people may seem, yet each one is aware of his/her destination.

Such destination route must have been booked online prior to the fellow's visit to the airport so what the fellow does, on arrival at the airport are;

- Pay attention to airline's name/identity
- Pay attention to airline's destination
- Pay attention to airline's flight time
- Pay attention to his/her personal luggage, etc.

After a while, the aircraft company's ushers approaches the passengers' stand; the first thing they usually ask each one is;

What is your destination?

I am asking you same question, what is your destination?

You must, from your self-discovery begin to pay attention to your destination in terms of life journey.

Will you board cab, say a commercial cab, and the driver is asking for your destination so he could, program the GPS to soothe your journey and correspond with your destination. Then your reply is anywhere? Anywhere leads nowhere!

In working out [and working at] your destination in life, the following tips will be necessary:

- Define your destination (**be sure**)
- Design your destination (**the planning**)
- Descript your destination (**exact picture**)
- Determine your destination (**be passionate)**
- Deployment to your destiny (**final movement to actualize your dreams**)

Day 23

Topic: BORN GREAT III

"The Place of Association"

Your association determines your relegation or celebration.

Have you discovered great people always associate with great people like them?

Start from your school, it doesn't matter the level of your school fees - it's likely people of the same financial class are those whose children attend the same school.

Have you also noticed when you watch celebrity hangout, you must discover stars hangout with stars.

When stars hangout with stars - none stars among them are never noticed.

The only way the none-star among the gathering of stars is noticed is when any among the stars introduces the none-star.

Even at then, people won't get interested, until several other times when such none star's face become familiar for as long as such is able to hangout among stars. When you look out in the skies, the only objects you can notice are whatever shines brighter - such is the nature of association. Now let's drive this home.

You have made self-discovering

You have planned your destination

Who are those that make up your association?

Those in your association will determine:

- When you get to your destination
- How you get to your destination
- If you ever get to your destination

Think about the above wisdom nuggets carefully, they mean a lot to your life journey, as mediocre or trail blazer!

Day 24

Topic: BORN GREAT IV

"Associational Dispositions"

WHEN = what time you arrive

Have you ever gone out with one of your friends and you find such greeting everyone he/she knows on the way.

Not only that, while on the same outing, the fellow kept asking, please let me use this opportunity to see this person and that person, etc.

And you don't want to overreact in the name of friendship [and for the sake of friendship], so you won't be viewed a puff-up.

My dear youngster, to embark on a journey with such people, you must be prepared to waste your time.

A time waster it's also a life waster, because time is the sum total of life hence you must have been familiar with the term "lifetime"

HOW = circumstances surrounding your arrival

Let's take it from where we stopped. For instance, that same friend you both went out. Even though you already planned your destination, but here you are, with someone who is lousy, who wants everyone to notice him/her in your company or that you're both on a cab or your parent's ride, etc.

Such type of lousy friend could insult or say what is capable of provoking a fight with someone else (while on the journey with you) and you won't want to abandon your so-called friend!

Outing with such lousy friend may land you both in a quarrel or fight with other hot-tempered folks; and before you know it, it has resulted into a fight. Before you know it, your both clothes are torn in such drama, etc.

You are getting to your destination, but in torn clothes, [within just one outing]?

IF = possibility of getting there

With the two experiences I have shared with you so far, don't you think the possibility of arriving at your destination in the company of such friend is slim?

Haven't you heard of people who set out on a planned journey, but someone they lifted on their way, suddenly developed a sort of sickness, which landed them first in the hospital, and later mortuary.

Have you also heard of someone who insisted his entire family attend a friend's wedding? They never arrive at the wedding neither did they return home, why?

They had accident on the way going and all died. When you refuse to chose your association carefully, such is what to expect.

One fact about association is that it is capable of progressing or retrogressing one's life, career, academics, etc. This is why one of the ancient books said – "association is contagious."

TODAY

IS

REVISION

Day 25th

Topic: ***HOW GREAT PEOPLE LIVE***

Now that you have learnt few things that could become impediments to you or in your quest for greatness.

Of which I believe you will put up a resistance!

It's usually much more better to let you know what great people do – knowing where you want to be and learning from those who have been there [before you make the decision to go there],going to live there and learning from those who are already living there are not the same.

This is why, every living or past champion knows the importance of skilful coach.

Where you may ask - the answer is experience! Having come this far to learn certain things about world's greatest fellows, I will also like to show you few secrets of the world's greatest.

Self-identification

Great people thrive in what they do more than average people do because; the first clarity they check out is on the issue of identity. **"To lack personal identity is to end up a nonentity"**

Creative /productive thinkers

Great people create time to think unlike average people who create time to talk and talk. Those who talk too much can't keep secret because they have loosed-mouth. Those who spend time to think, from time to time, are better off because they think on what to say before talking. It will take a degree of creative/productive thinking to generate solution for challenging situation per time. **Humanity is a product of a thinker. God's thought gave birth to the universe and humanity! Therefore, if God is a thinker, we humans are equally, expected to be human-thinkers!**

Ideas generation

You must have heard about the phrase, "ideas rule the world"

What this simple means is – whatever we make use of today was part of someone's idea's generation, yesterday. Every idea generation came into light because of man's endless desires. Ever before the conception of an idea is conceived in a certain part of the world, there must have been the need for such (in another part of the world). Ideas generation is naturally, motivated by wants. They are like Siamese twins.

Ideas generation = eradication of human needs/wants.

Passion oriented

Every vision without genuine passion will end up as illusion!

Great people are passionate about almost everything they do.

Donald Trump said –

"Very often, the dividing line between success and failure is passion. Without passion in place, fantastic idea may eventually end up as fantastic failure"

Passion is the inherent zeal behind the pursuit of a vision, etc. Persistent passion is what gives you your portion despite the resistance of opposition and stiff competition! **You can't stop a genuine passionate individual – such is prepared to die for whatever he is determined to live for!**

DAY 26

Topic: **HOW GREAT PEOPLE THINK**

Information acquisition

Here is the major disparity between the rich and the poor – information!

While the poor lives on assumption, the rich leverage on information. Information is the ability to remain current, especially in your line of interest, career, etc. An informed student will always be ahead of his peers - those who have information are leaders, but those without information queue behind, you cannot separate information from greatness. Good a thing we are in such era, the of information age.

Tenacity

You must have heard of **Thomas Edison**'s testimony. How he maintained tenacity before discovering the electric bulb. He tried 999 times, until the circle completed a thousand, then his persistency worth the while.

Quality takes time to achieve. Whatever is done often in a hurry does not usually come out best - but the best comes up much later. People of tenacity are those with the fighting spirit. They seldom give up on whatever they venture into doing.

Time Managers

Great people define their time. They do not just define it, but they also take a step further to plan it out. You cannot become great, or maintain greatness without understanding the relevance of time.

The summary of your age is the summary of the time you have spent on earth. This is why you always notice the use of the world "LIFETIME", the best use of time is the ability to focus on what matter most to you in life per time!

"You value for time determine the value you get with time – from time to time"

The truth is - no one can manage time effectively, what great people do often is, they manage themselves to soothe the time allocated to them.

Success Mindset

"Great people think success even before becoming successful"

You can take my word to the bank. I have not discussed imagination with you since the beginning of this book, maybe I will in the next volume.

Imagination is not just the ability to see far off like vision, it's the ability to see the future with a possibility mentality.

This is why it's good you learn the act of possibility thinking by associating with those who have already become what you also is aspiring to become.

Great people just imagine good things, favour, fortune, etc. Somehow, nature allows such thoughts become realities. The same way nature and humans breathe into each other, so also nature responds to the imagination of man.

What you say and imagine from time to time is capable of attracting what your experience is in life.

I could remember some years ago, my first child [**God's wealth** by name], while in the higher institution, she said a time came for a particular test. While others were registering, she lacked the fund required. Therefore, she imagined that such test was postponed until she was ready; through to her imagination, the test was postponed - with no student understanding why!

You can`t develop the mindset of success and think you will end up a failure in life – that is impossible! Imagination is the human ability to stretch his mental reasoning beyond his physical senses, circumstances and physical environments – via possibility thinking!

Day 27
Topic: BEHAVE YOUR MINDSET

There is no way I could have closed up this chapter without letting you know about mindset. There is a law in physiology; one of such is The Law of cause and effect.

The lame understanding for such is popularly called: sowing and reaping.

I want to teach you one of the actions of great people`s mindset. Such wish others well, and from their heart. It doesn`t really matter if they have close relationship with the individual the wish well – they just wish such well!

Wishing people well is a seed, as you sow such – one day you too shall be, wished well!

Take a ride around beautiful places, snap photos there, look out beautiful homes, read about successful people, and admire gorgeous cars. Bless the people that owns such things from your heart – a day is coming that such is going to be your experience.

E-mail or send letters to the successful people you know, wishing them well and congratulating them for exploits they have accomplished.

One of Nigeria's university founders told us; several years ago, he visited America to see the beauty and glamour surrounding **Oral Robert University**. After going around and blessing the founder from his heart. He said on that ground while admiring the institution:

"This is God - but it can happen anywhere in the world!"

About two decades after, that man also has become the proud founder of two tertiary institutions - **Covenant University** and **Landmark University**!

The law of attraction says - what you are attracted to, is what you attract in return.

Nevertheless, I must warn you to mind your attractions, because we are only talking about positive attraction here!

Day 28

Topic: **ASSET OR LIABILITY**

Nigeria is a liability nation because we depend on importation to the point even we import tooth pick, yes!

Possibly, because we are not fortunate to have creative & productive thinking leaders, hence Nigeria will keep on depending on other nations for surviving. My question is what if such nations become economically challenged just as China is presently challenged with **Corona virus**. That means Nigeria is definitely going to become grounded, economically (God forbid).

In the light of the above, you must decide to become an asset and not a liability.

There are juveniles out there who have already turned out to become assets to their nations. Someone, like, Mark Zukerberg - Face book founder

The foundation for asset mentality begins from your individual:

- Perception
- Perspective
- Conviction

- Determination
- Decision

Only you posses the right over the above highlights, as regards your personal life

Let me lead you all over, from the bottom rung of the ladder.

Decision

From age eighteen, you have the sole right to develop your personal decision for your future. When I say you have the right – eighteen is the legal age where maturity begins in Nigeria. This does not have to stop you from forming good, productive decisions before you attain such age.

With what I have inculcated into you from the inception of this book-what is your decision - success or failure?

Determination

You can understand determination from mountain climbers view. Once they set out from the bottom of the mountain, they are prepared to die climbing until they reach the top. It does not matter whether mountain snakes or scorpion crawl across their part- they are determined!

You must determine to succeed in life by doing what is demanded of you, in accordance to the legal rules that already let others through such part of life! Such includes taking appropriate steps cum prompt personal responsibility.

Conviction

Success or failure is a matter of confusion or conviction. You are either convinced or confused; you cannot stand on the fence. You must be convinced that you too were born great just like others who are sharing the stories of greatness, and with the world applauding them from time to time.

Great people become great by solving problems. You can also start solving problems as a teenage or young adult – you can start with your school, win a price, create invention, initiate a saleable idea, etc. You must be convinced that you're created a change agent – and not a bunch of liability [in your mentality].

Perspective

Perspective talks about your pattern of doing things, which is because of your pattern of reasoning. Your definition of how things ought to be. You're not just subscribing to what is in vogue, knowing that the generality of humanity is made of ignorance. Your perspective should be based on:

- Thinking right
- Behaving right
- Living right
- Creating right solutions, etc.

Your way of doing things differently is as a result of viewing things differently – from the right perspective.

Perception

Your perception is ability to capture unpopular information from the mental realm. This requires consistency in reading and researching culture. You can't be a genius without enjoying the atmosphere of robust perception. Inventors and innovators are people of great perception. Creative and productive thinking will always culminate in profitable perception.

A juvenile or youthful mind must be concerned with how to convert such potential into assets without conversion; such is bound to end up poor!

Asset oriented personalities are those whose dexterity, dignity and qualities metamorphoses into authorities in their fields – people in such field cannot be pushed over.

You cannot possess the above attributes in your self-development practice and not emerge one of the national pathfinders - of economic success stories in your nation.

Day 29

Topic: THE PLACE OF CHARACTER

In the course of my administration of training for leaders, young adults and juvenile, I have observed very few youths are able to survive at the top when they become famous or successful.

Charisma may introduce you, but it will take a great degree of personal character for you to be sustained, at the top of whatever career you find yourself in life. The limit of your character will determine the height of your placement in life.

- Character is what you think, with no one knowing
- Character is what you do secretly, with no one seeing.
- Character is your attitude when you are offended
- Character, just like the titanic ship builders said, "Even God cannot sink it"; it exposes your weakness - during your pick of enthusiasm.
- Character is the anchor that helps the ship survives any storm – it holds firmly!
- Character clarity determines what gravity of weight or that of challenges you can sustain in life per time.

Two things will help you sustain your true character [that is if you have such]:

- Self-identity – knowing who you are

- Self discipline - fighting to defend who you`re

Day 30

Topic: **LEARNING: HIGHEST PRIORITY**

A wise man once said, "when you stop learning, you'll start dying " (paraphrased)

Knowledge is the largest room in the world [I suppose]. Knowledge is inexhaustible. You cannot come to a point in life (neither had anyone ever], where you can boast and say; I have all the knowledge, or I have already known all.

Actually, a certain portion in one of the holy books says:

"To think you already know what you ought to know simply means - you are yet to know all you ought to know"

My dear youngster ambassador, the reason I advise you to learn more is because you are yet to access what you ought to have known, even at your young age, and in your academics, or career. There is nothing, no knowledge; that somewhere or someone around the world has not created, as record, or achieved as feat!

Nevertheless, you can break such record, only when you are able to go beyond such record's creation and creator's knowledge arsenals.

Achieving such feat will require some more investments and diligence, such as

- Make learning your highest
- Positioning your nose in books daily
- Avoiding unproductive friends
- Determine to beat your last grades
- Competing with academically achieved role models - in line with your career
- Avoid unsavoury characters
- Invest additional time for extracurricular activities, etc.

TODAY

IS

REVISION

Available on Amazon.com
KINGS
WAY
...Youths in the foot steps of kings

Dynamics
OF
Leadership
...unveiling leadership mental dynamism...
Dominion Oluyadi

Available on Amazon.com
360 DEGREES
ENTREPRENEUR
1st. business devotional in Africa!
business productivity in tangible reality!
...business-leadership devotional

DOMINION OLUYADI
Vol.1
JUVENILE
CHARACTER
DEVOTIONAL
...solution to juvenile deliquency!
(+daily ettiquette)

7 IDENTITY
OF EAGLE'S
MENTALITY
....Soaring via productive mentality
Dominion Oluyadi

POLITICAL LEADERS'
CHARACTER
Devotional
...developing next level attitude in politics!
by
Dominion Oluyadi
Available on Amazon.com
1st political devotional in Africa!

CHARACTER
DRIVEN
LIFE
...your way through life via character values!
Dominion Oluyadi

TRUMP
TOWER
DONALD-TRUMP'S
MENTALITY
Dominion Oluyadi

THE AMBASSADORS

...solution to juvenile delinquency!

The eagle has a special character when compared to other birds. The eagle controls its relationship by selecting the friends. The eagle does not feed on left over, neither will it consider feasting on dead prey - no matter the degree of hunger. The eagle possess royalty mentality, hence, it will never consider casual sex until legal marriage is consummated

In the same vein, The Ambassadors Devotional chronicles a mental reorientation for teenagers /young adults generally.

The fact is, the quality of the world's future depends largely on youth mental capacity/exploration via productive thinking - because youths are the future of the world! This edition is out to re-brand the brain of the juvenile!

Dominion Oluyadi
best selling author
of
31 laws of character

3252 9586 84813

MIX
Papier aus verantwortungsvollen Quellen
Paper from responsible sources
FSC® C105338

Printed by Books on Demand GmbH, Norderstedt / Germany